Bark Carving

by Joyce Buchanan

Fox
Chapel Publishing Co. Inc.
1970 Broad Street • East Petersburg, PA 17520 • www.foxchapelpublishing.com

Publisher: Alan Giagnocavo
Project Editor: Ayleen Stellhorn
Desktop Specialist: Robert Altland, Altland Design, Lancaster, PA
Photographers: Ray McDonald, St. Albert, Alberta
Don Spooner "Prints," Edmonton, Alberta

ISBN # 1–56523–132–5

To order your copy of this book, please
send check or money order for cover price
plus $3.50 to:
Fox Chapel Book Orders
1970 Broad Street
East Petersburg, PA 17520

www.foxchapelpublishing.com

Try your Favorite book supplier first!

Printed in China

10 9 8 7 6 5 4 3 2

Table of Contents

Projects and Patterns

This book is dedicated to
Tony Wispinski who first "introduced"
me to Cottonwood Spirits;
my special friends
who found bark for me;
and those who accompanied me
on bark-hunting expeditions.

CHAPTER 1

Introduction to Carving Bark

Through long years, the Cottonwood Spirits have guarded all living things within the shadows of their tree.

Now that their old trees have died, they're willing to emerge.

For those who value and preserve Nature, may these Cottonwood Spirits bring you long life, happiness, and protection.

Just what happens to a Cottonwood tree's spirit when the tree dies? Some believe it can be relocated and depicted in the bark to bring pleasure to the carver and owner.

Some rather unique bark carvings from early Alberta times were called Bannock gods. They emerged, under the carver's knife, to see that the little children ate their bannock, a "biscuit-like" flat bread. In European history, little faces were carved from bark to ward off undesirable spirits, bring good luck, and help to keep households safe. The Inuit, native North Americans who live in northern areas of Canada and Alaska, carved likenesses of the creatures they hunted and with which they were familiar.

After taking a short course in bark carving from Tony Wispinski, I found that I was

Introduction

delighted with the little faces that "emerged" from the bark. I, too, like so many others before me, was entranced by the spirits of the trees.

As I carve, I give a "personality" to my work by naming the tree spirit. Tony calls his bark carvings "Wispy's Whimsys." I call mine "Cottonwood Spirits."

I do not use a plan or even consciously decide the type of face each of my bark carvings will have. The faces seem to be there—just waiting for me to remove the excess bark and find them.

Patterns are helpful, however, especially for beginning carvers. I have included many in this book. Of course, each will probably need to be altered slightly to fit each unique piece of bark. This can be easily accomplished by finding the pattern most suited to the shape of the bark and altering some of the Cottonwood Spirit's features. You can also make your own patterns by using the illustrations of facial features in Chapter 4 to "build" your own pattern for a Cottonwood Spirit.

You will enjoy the ease with which the bark can be carved. To get you started, I have included basic information on the various tools used in bark carving, general carving instructions, and several step-by-step carving demonstrations. I've also included a chapter on common bark-carving problems and how to solve them.

The faces of my Cottonwood Spirits are imaginary, and realism is only an illusion! Strict adherence to symmetry and correct anatomy is unnecessary, unless you wish otherwise. For those of you who would like to know more about how the human face is structured, I have included a section describing the anatomical features of the face. This section will give you background knowledge; you'll want to refer to your own face in the mirror and collect or sketch pictures of unique and interesting faces as reference material.

It is my wish that through this book, you, too, will find real carving enjoyment as you "release" the spirits of the trees. I do hope that you will derive as much satisfaction from carving bark as I do!

Above all... Relax! Enjoy! And avoid cutting yourself!

CHAPTER 2

Basic Tools for Carving Bark

Basic Bark-Carving Tools

Carving Knife*
Leather Strop*
Sharpening Compound*
Assorted Gouges*
Wire Brush*
Calipers
Old Tooth Brush*
Permanent Black Marker*
Sandpaper*
Rubber Fingers
Soft Pencil*
Paper*
Hand Mirror
Bench Hook*
Acrylic Paints
Paint Brushes
Hand Towel*
Wood Glue
Elastic Bands
Wood Filler
Drill Bit
Smoothing Plane
Protective Pouch*

The bark-carving tools listed at left are for those carvers who prefer to use hand tools. You may carve bark using just a jack knife or a carving knife, however, a few special gouges and other tools greatly add to the enjoyment. Some of the items listed at the left are optional. The basic essentials are marked with an asterisk.

Power tools may be used, though I find that I enjoy working the bark with hand tools. If you do use power tools, be sure to maintain good ventilation and use a dust collector.

1. Before you make a cut, ask yourself, "If I slip, will I cut myself?" If the answer is yes, then move your hands so a slip doesn't result in an injury.

2. Hold and support the bark behind your carving tool. Always work away from yourself.

3. Keep your tools sharp.

Tools

Carving Knife

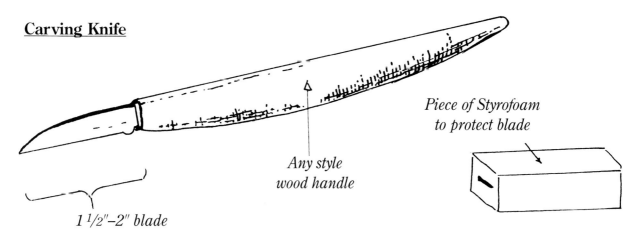

*Any style
wood handle*

*Piece of Styrofoam
to protect blade*

1 1/2"–2" blade

Choose a knife with a comfortable handle and a short blade (about 1¹/₂"). A short blade is easier to use in small spaces; it allows the carver to use a "whittling" technique and to push the blade with a finger or thumb of the opposite hand. If the knife does not have a protective cover, push the blade into a block of styrofoam when it is not in use.

Leather Strop

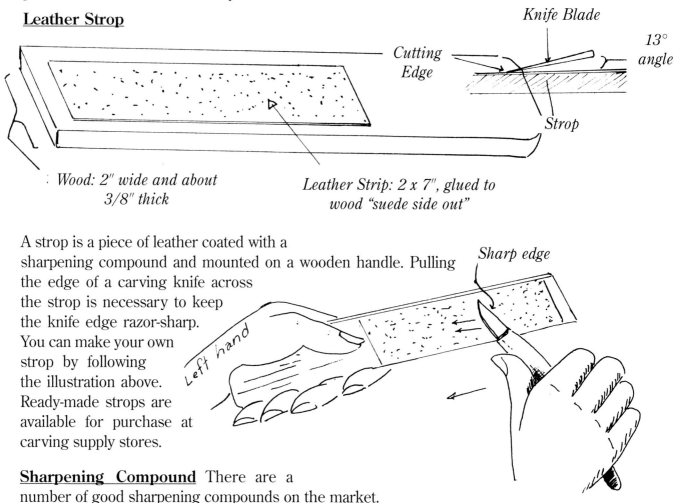

Knife Blade

*Cutting
Edge*

*13°
angle*

Strop

*Wood: 2" wide and about
3/8" thick*

*Leather Strip: 2 x 7", glued to
wood "suede side out"*

A strop is a piece of leather coated with a sharpening compound and mounted on a wooden handle. Pulling the edge of a carving knife across the strop is necessary to keep the knife edge razor-sharp. You can make your own strop by following the illustration above. Ready-made strops are available for purchase at carving supply stores.

Sharp edge

Left hand

Sharpening Compound
There are a number of good sharpening compounds on the market.
Rub or "shave" a small amount onto the suede side of the leather strop. Strop the knife by pulling the blade toward you with the sharp edge trailing. Then turn the blade over and push away from you. Frequent stroppings will keep the blade sharp.

4

Gouges*

Choose gouges with handles that provide a comfortable grip.

Vee Gouge—75° 4.5 mm*
Use a v-gouge to define the sides of the nose, the arch of the eyebrows, the shape of the upper eyelids, the beginning cuts under the nose, the line between the lips, and the lines in the hair, eyebrows, mustache, and beard.

V-Gouge or Parting Gouge—60° angle, 1.5 mm or 3 mm
Use this smaller v-gouge in the same instances as the larger v-gouge, but on a smaller face. This tool will achieve more delicate detail.

Small 3 mm Round Gouge
Use a small round gouge to shape small, flat areas, to work around the lips and curls of hair, and to clean out the nostrils.

Flattened Round Gouge—10 mm
A flattened round gouge is used on larger faces to shape small,flat areas, to work around the lips and curls of hair, and to clean out nostrils.

Very Shallow Round Gouge—16 mm*
This very versatile gouge is used to shape the eyebrows, the curves of the eye-balls, the curved lines under the eyes, the top curves of the cheeks, the sides of the nose, and the curve of the upper lip. It is also used to shape the general contour of the beard and hair and to clean the back of the bark.

Straight Gouge—12 mm*
Use a straight gouge to clean the surface bark from the area where the face will appear. This tool is also used to shape the top line of the nose and the nostril edge and to contour the cheeks, mustache, and beard.

Skew Gouge—about 7 mm*
This tool is ideal for shaping the bridge of the nose and the eyes. It also works well when defining corners and straight cuts in conjunction with a carving knife.

Wire Brush

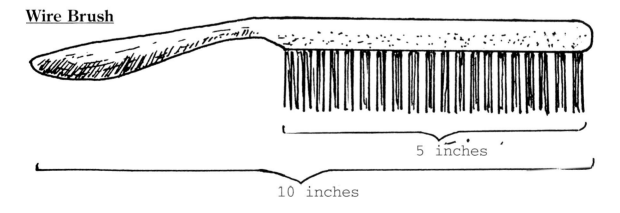

5 inches

10 inches

A wire brush can be purchased from a hardware store. It is used to clean the bark.

Tools

Calipers

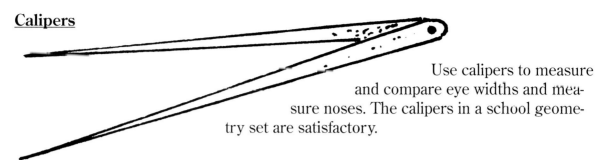

Use calipers to measure and compare eye widths and measure noses. The calipers in a school geometry set are satisfactory.

Old Tooth Brush An old toothbrush is handy to brush away small pieces of bark from the area being carved.

Permanent Black Marker Sign your name and date on the back of each carving with a permanent marker. You may also wish to number your carvings. Be sure to pre-test the marker on a piece of scrap bark to ensure your finish will not make the ink run.

Sandpaper

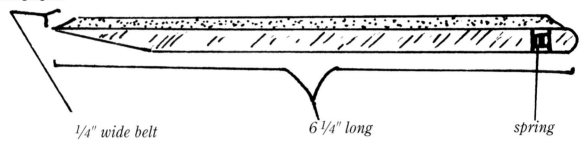

¼" wide belt   *6 ¼" long*   *spring*

Use a 220 or finer grit sandpaper; coarse sandpaper will scratch the soft bark. I find that cloth- or polyester-backed sandpaper is easier to use than paper-backed sandpaper. Sanding sticks with sandpaper belts, such as the one shown above, are very convenient as they allow precise sanding of narrow areas. The colors of the handles indicate the grit (ie: Brown - 600 grit, Yellow - 400 grit, Green - 320 grit, Blue - 220 grit). Emery boards make useful sanders as well. A piece of sandpaper cut to fit around the cork from a wine bottle, shown at right, will make the sandpaper easier to grasp.

cork —

sandpaper wrapped
around cork

Rubber Fingers Rubber fingers come in different sizes and are commonly used by postal employees, bank clerks, and secretaries to facilitate the handling of paper. For carvers, they make good finger "protectors," especially if you wish to push on the back of the knife blade as you carve away from yourself.

A Soft Pencil Use a soft-leaded pencil, either 3B or 4B will work well, to draw details on the bark.

Paper Keep paper handy to sketch ideas as you carve or to make new patterns.

A Hand Mirror One of the best sources of reference material is your own face.

Bench Hook

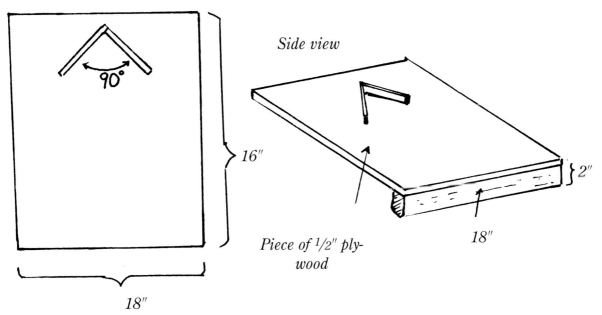

Top view

Side view

90°

16″

18″

2″

18″

Piece of ¹/₂″ ply-wood

A bench hook is a home-made device constructed to "hold" the wood so that it does not move as you carve. The bench hook allows you to apply considerable pressure with gouges, a plane, or a knife as you carve and remove the back material. The bench hook that I use is pictured above, but dimensions will vary depending on your project and your work space.

Acrylic Paints If you wish to paint the eyes, use acrylic Artists' colors: Paynes Grey, White, Burnt Sienna. Use Raw Sienna to paint over filled worm canals.

Paint Brushes Use a very small round brush, #1 or #2, to paint the eyes.

Old Hand Towel Lay your tools on the towel so that the edges and points do not touch. Arrange the tools so that they point away from you and so that you can pick them up without risk of a cut.

Carpenters' Glue, Wood Filler Use these materials to fill cracks or worm canals.

Drill Bit

A ³/₁₆ inch drill bit inserted into a pear shaped wooden handle. Any type of handle that will hold the bit is satisfactory. This tool will enable you to easily make the hole in the back of the finished bark carving so that the carving can be hung on the wall. It may also be used, on larger carvings, to "clean out" the inside of the nostrils and make the indentation for the eye's pupil (if you make pupils that way).

Drill a hole the same circumference as the bit and press the bit into the handle

Tools

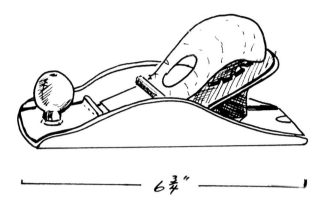

6¾"

Small Smoothing Plane   Use a plane to remove and finish the back if the bark is quite thick. I have a small antique plane that looks like the one pictured above. Modern planes are sold at hardware stores. Anyone who sharpens knives can sharpen a plane for you.

Protective Pouch

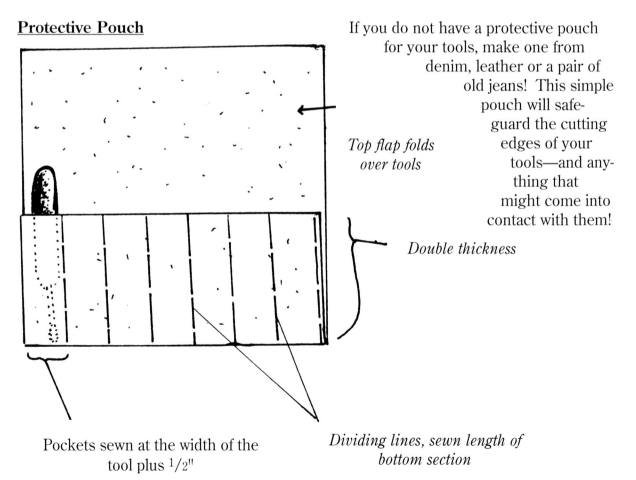

If you do not have a protective pouch for your tools, make one from denim, leather or a pair of old jeans! This simple pouch will safe-guard the cutting edges of your tools—and any-thing that might come into contact with them!

Top flap folds over tools

Double thickness

Pockets sewn at the width of the tool plus 1/2"

Dividing lines, sewn length of bottom section

CHAPTER 3

Finding Cottonwood Bark

The Cottonwood tree is also known as Balsam Poplar, Black Poplar, Black Cottonwood, balm of Gilead, Rough-barked Popular, and Tacamahac. It is a tree of medium size displaying very "ribbed" bark.

The Black Cottonwood may be found from Alaska south, through Western Canada, Washington, central and northern Idaho, western Montana, northern and western Oregon, northern California and the Baja California Peninsula.

The Eastern Cottonwood extends east from the Black Cottonwood's range. It is prevalent in river valleys of southern Alberta and Saskatchewan (Canada), western North Dakota, most areas of South Dakota, Nebraska, Kansas, Oklahoma, Arkansas, Missouri, Iowa, eastern Texas, northern Louisiana, Mississippi, Alabama (except in isolated areas), much of Georgia, central and eastern South Carolina, central North Carolina, central and southern Minnesota

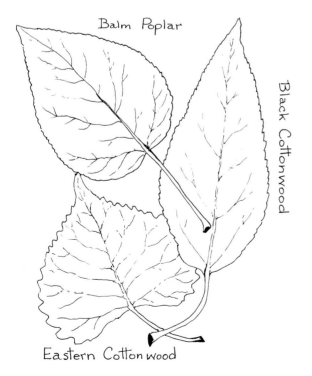

Balm Poplar

Black Cottonwood

Eastern Cottonwood

Finding Cottonwood Bark

and Michigan, Indiana, Ohio, and Illinois. Isolated areas also occur in Virginia, West Virginia, Maryland, Pennsylvania, New York, Vermont, New Hampshire, Massachusetts, and Connecticut, northern and western Kentucky, and central and western Tennessee.

There is also a Cottonwood tree specific to isolated areas of California, Arizona, New Mexico, Utah, Colorado, and western Texas known as the Freemont Cottonwood.

The Narrowleaf Cottonwood extends in isolated areas from Idaho south, through Utah, New Mexico, and into central Arizona.

The Arizona Cottonwood is found in isolated areas of Arizona, central New Mexico, and western Texas. (Reference: Little, E.L.,

This is a fine example of a Balsam Popular. It is over one hundred years old with an approximate circumference of fifteen feet at the base. This tree is still alive, and of course, one would not try to remove the bark! Someday, when it dies, the bark will make good carving material.

Bark may be removed easily, either with one's bare hands or by using a pry-bar.

Finding Cottonwood Bark

Jr. 1979, *Atlas of United States Trees.* U.S. Dept. of Agriculture For. Serv. Washington, D.C. Misc. Publ. 1146, Volumes One and Three.)

To find suitable Cottonwood bark, look for an old, large, dead tree or its stump. The tree may be fifty to one hundred feet tall and two to four feet in diameter. (The bigger the better!) Stumps are usually found in river valleys or in close proximity to plentiful water supplies. Start your search in areas that have old stands of trees where no logging has taken place—or at least a minimal amount. Remember to ask permission if the area is on private property, and never leave any signs of your presence—whether you're on private *or* public land.

The wood of a Cottonwood tree is considered "soft" and not very highly regarded. You may be aware of the tree's fruit capsules in the late spring when they burst open and fill the air with cotton "fluff." The leaf covers fall to the ground and stick to shoes and pets' feet. However, though this tree can be a problem, please do not take bark from a live tree! Removing the bark leaves the tree defenseless against disease and insects.

Bark on a dead tree's trunk is usually easy to remove. Just grasp a rib and pull. Sometimes I've had to pry the bark off with a tire iron, rock-hammer pick, or long screw driver. But, if the bark is dry and the tree is completely dead, the bark should come off easily.

When you collect your own bark, many ribs will be fairly straight. Any with twists or bulges or any ribs fastened together offer an opportunity to carve a greater variety of faces.

You may wish to try other types of bark, but I've found that Cottonwood bark is the only type with real depth and solidity. Bark can be as thin as $1^{1}/2''$, but as a general rule of thumb, the thicker, the better.

Look for old dead Cottonwood tree stumps. These are usually found in riverbed areas, or near water sources where trees are very old.

Here's enough bark to provide carving material for many months!

CHAPTER 4

Anatomy of the Human Face

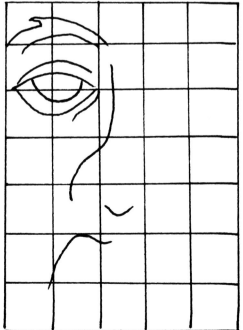

As I mentioned before, strict adherence to anatomical correctness need not be followed. However, I feel knowing more about the structure of the human face will help you to be more creative.

Along with anatomical notes on the human face, I have also included a series of eyes, noses, mouths, beards and mustaches in this chapter. You can create a new Cottonwood face by choosing the features you would like to carve and tracing them on a piece of paper. All of the illustrations are the same scale, so trace and construct a face directly on your paper.

The size of the face you carve depends on the dimensions of the piece of bark you use. The features illustrated here will fit a rib of bark that is at least $2^1/2''$ wide.

To enlarge or reduce the face to fit your bark, try using a photocopier, re-drawing the face freehand, or using the grid method pictured here.

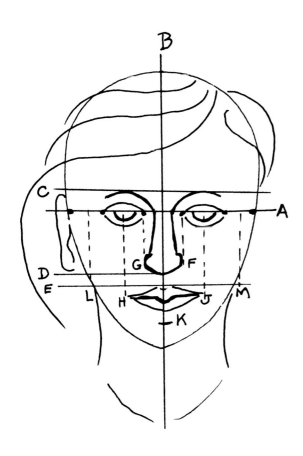

Proportions of an Adult Face

The following 12 points are generalizations. There is great variety among human faces. (Look at the model in your mirror.) These basics are simply meant to help you "plan" a face.

1. The corners of the eyes should be no higher than line A.

2. Divide line A (face areas) into five equal parts. Mark with dots.

3. The bridge of the nose fits between the center two dots. (It only uses up half the space.)

4. Draw the eyes in the two sections on either side of the bridge of the nose.

5. Draw the eyebrows just above the eyes (above line A). The highest part of them is line C.

6. The nose is one to one-and-one-half the width of the eye.

7. Divide the center line B in half between the eyes and the chin (line E). This line is the top of the top lip. Draw the lips below it.

8. Extend the inner corners of the eyes downward. The outer edges of the nostrils lie on these lines (lines G and F).

9. The corners of the mouth are straight below the centers of the eye-pupils (lines H and J).

10. An indentation below the bottom lip is one-third of the distance to the chin (line K).

11. Ears extend from the bottom of the nose (line D) to the eye socket (between lines A and C).

12. Divide the two outside fifths of line A in half. Extend a line downward. The neck joins the face in about that area (lines L and M).

If you wish to become proficient at drawing faces, practice diligently! As models, use yourself, your friends, good photographs, and art books. To capture a "likeness," you must learn to observe carefully. Let me say again, however, that when carving Cottonwood Spirits many of the measurements and real proportions may be changed and exaggerated due to the limiting proportions of the bark ribs and your own creativity.

Anatomy

Eyes and Eyebrows

The human eye is comparable to a ping-pong ball with a slight bulge over the pupil area. It fits into the eye socket. The eyebrow line flows smoothly down over the eyelid with a slight indentation over the pupil and then on to the cheek. Check the shape and contour of your own eyes using the mirror.

Study your bark carefully. The widest part of the bark will often suggest the width of the eye area. Sometimes a lot of upper eyelid shows if the eyeball protrudes, but if it is recessed into the socket, only a small amount of eyelid may be visible. You may wish to carve both upper and lower eyelids, only the upper lids, or no eyelids at all.

On the opposite page are some eye shapes and eyebrow suggestions. They are the same scale as the noses, beards, and mustaches, so continue to trace until you have combined the features in a face that appeals to you.

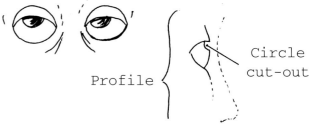

Top: A straight cut is used to make eyes that appear to be downcast. Bottom: Pupils can be made by cutting out a circle with a gouge, knife, or drill bit.

14

Eyes

Eyebrows

Anatomy

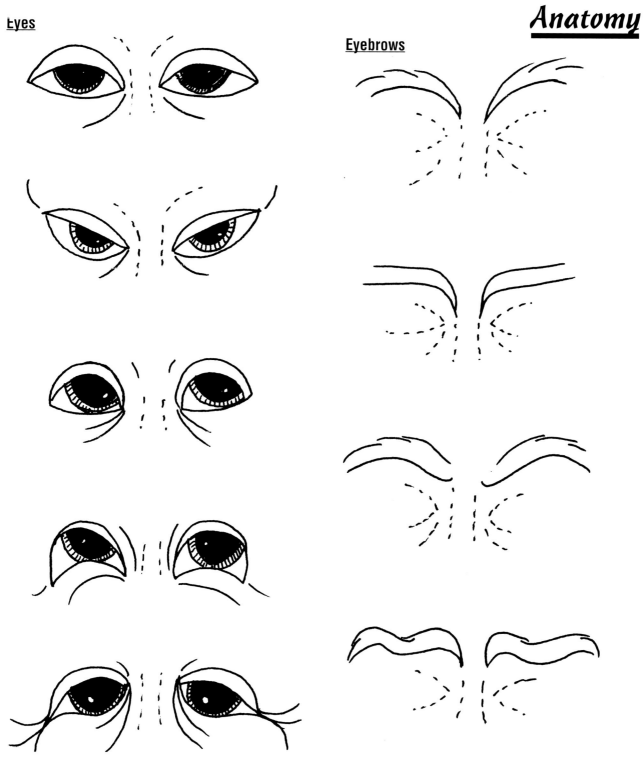

You may wish to make a shallow cut along the top eyelid line to remove a small amount of bark over the pupil area. Pupils may be defined in any way you wish or not shown at all. Here are three suggestions:
1) Outline the edge of the pupil with the v-gouge; 2) Cut a hole for the pupil as in Greek and Roman sculpture; 3) Paint the pupil on the eye surface with acrylic paints or felt pen.

The first eyebrow illustration is the easiest because it is made with downward pressure of the very shallow round gouge (16 mm). Its contour is the same as that of the gouge. The others may be carved with a v-gouge or knife.

15

Anatomy

Noses

Noses

The basic shape of a nose is a triangle. Modify this shape to include a nostril area when you draw it on the bark.

A suggested length for a nose would be one to $1\frac{1}{2}$ eye-widths. Children's noses are often one eye width in length. Of course, this is rather arbitrary as the nose length depends on the shape of the bark and the "personality" you are creating.

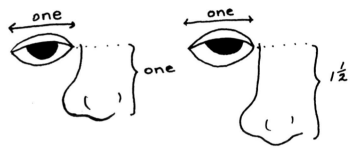

Nostrils slope from the tip of the nose to the cheek area. Refer to your own nose in a mirror. Slope the nostrils down toward the face from the tip of the nose. Curve the nostril area along the cheek line.

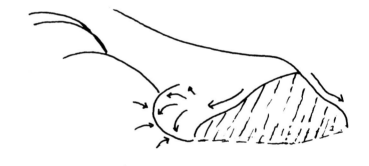

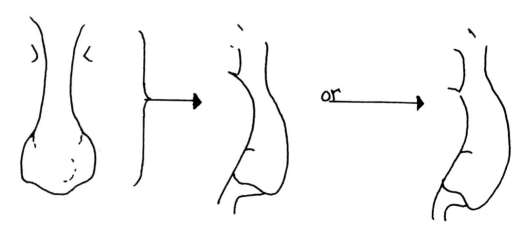

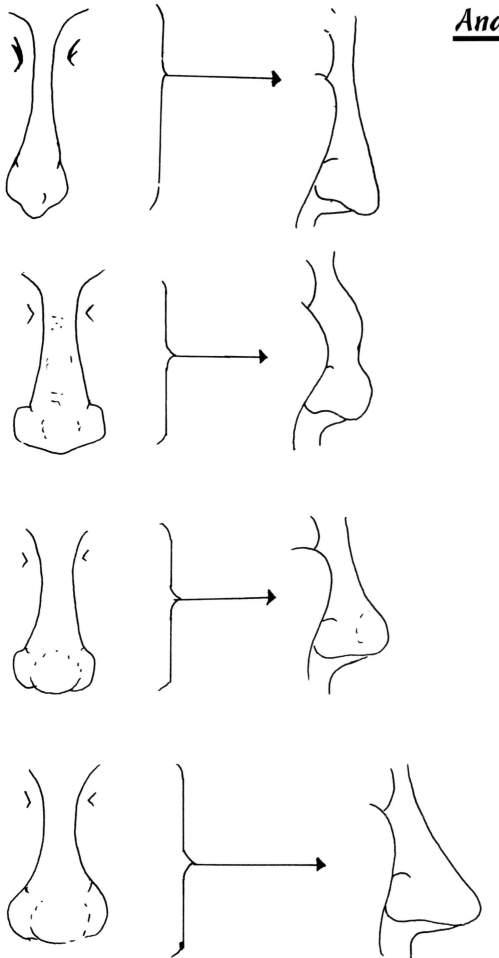

Anatomy

Lips and Mouths
Beards and Mustaches

Unless you have elected the severity of a very "firm," straight line, do curve the top lip along the mouth-line.

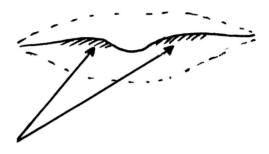

Cut a bit deeper under the top curves. Curve a woman's lips more than a man's.

The lines for the "flow" of the hair may be drawn and carved as close together as you wish. They may be straight, curved and flowing, or "kinky." Try to add interest by using a variety of line widths and lengths. Following the contours of the bark and allowing the lines to "flow" into cracks will also add interest.

The beard or mustache of one figure often can be allowed to flow into and become the hair of a second figure. Hair may also flow down to create the beard of a figure below.

Lips and Mouths

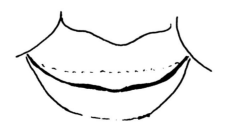

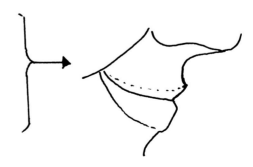

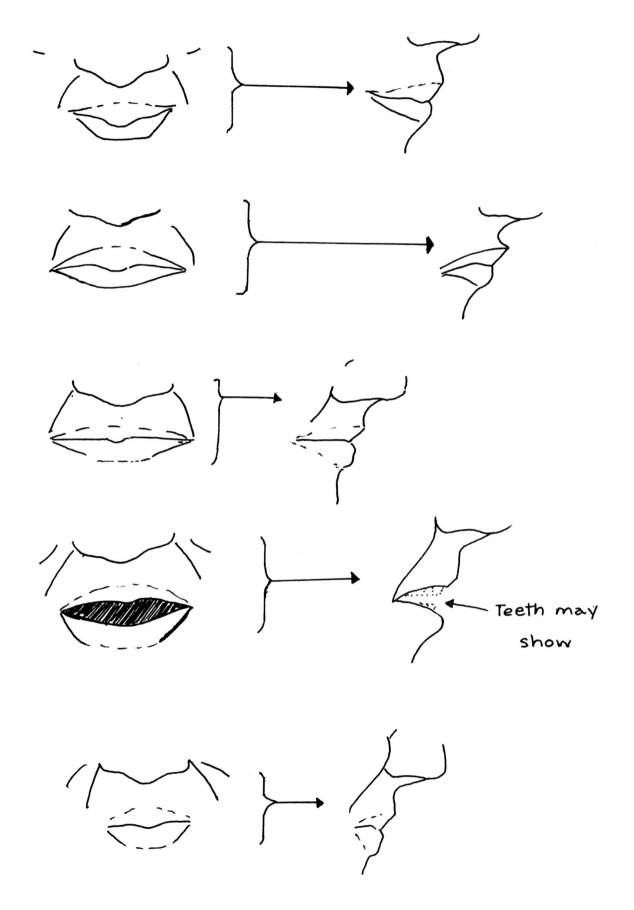

Teeth may show

Beards and Mustaches

CHAPTER 5

General Bark Carving Instructions

Before You Begin

1. Gather the tools you will need. Make sure that all the cutting edges are sharp; sharpen any tools that need it. Take care to keep sharp edges away from you.

2. Choose a comfortable working area with good light. Your work space should also have good ventilation, especially if you are working with power tools and varnishes or paints that have dangerous fumes.

3. Spend time planning the facial features you want to carve. You can combine the eye, nose, mouth, and beard illustrations from the previous chapter or alter one of the patterns in this book.

Preparing the Bark

1 Spread out your tools and place the bark in the bench hook on the table.

2 Using the wire brush, remove any loose material from the front of the bark. This will be the area where you carve the face. Also, brush away lichen and debris accumulated in the cracks.

3 Use a very shallow round gouge or a plane to clean the fibers and discoloration from the back of the bark (the side that was next to the wood of the tree). Use the bench hook to hold the bark steady as you do this. Work away from your hands until you have cleaned the entire surface to your satisfaction.

General Carving Instructions

The back of the bark usually has a concave surface. If you have thick bark, you may need to run it through a jointer, a motor-driven planer, to make it completely flat.

If you find any worm canals see page 27 for some solutions.

4 Have your pattern handy. Your pattern may be: (a) the one you developed using the features of your choice from Chapter 4; (b) a "character" face seen in a photo, book or magazine; (c) a face that the bark will "reveal" to you as you carve; or (d) one of the patterns in this book.

5 Keep the bark securely in the bench hook and use a flat gouge or a knife to remove the top surface of the front of the bark in the area where you wish to carve the face. You should remove enough bark to eliminate cracked bark and brittle or "flaking" bark. Remember, do not remove bark from the edge of the carving where you want some natural bark to frame the face.

If the bark has attractive patterns or colors in the grain, simplify the facial details to retain the bark's beauty.

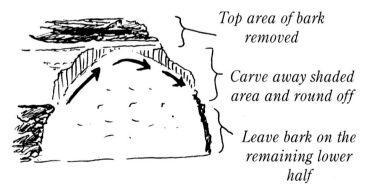

Top area of bark removed

Carve away shaded area and round off

Leave bark on the remaining lower half

6 Round the face area, working from the center to the outside edge. Don't be timid! Curve the sides until you have removed one-half the depth of the outside bark on the edge of the "rib." Think of the

face area as being one half of an orange. Faces are quite curved—the outer corner of the eye is much lower than the tip of the nose.

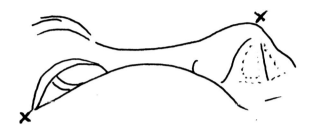

7 Using your drawing as a guide, pencil in lines on the bark to indicate: (a) an eyebrow line; (b) a triangular shaped nose; (c) the general shape of eyes; (d) a line for the mouth; and (e) a few lines for hair or beard.

8 Continue to work with the bark in the bench hook. Using the large v-gouge, cut in the lines along the side of the nose and across the eyebrows. Do not make the nose too narrow; remove the wood on the *outside* of your pencil marks. Deepen the gouge line with two or three more cuts. Always use two or more cuts to make a deep line; you may chip the work if you attempt to make a deep gouge with one cut.

9 Shape the line of the nose using a knife, straight gouge, or skew so you can see the nose profile you want. Lower the bridge of the nose to allow for the profile shape of the nose. Don't carve across the end of the nose yet.

10 Cut the eyebrows using the very shallow round gouge (16 mm). Then, cut the outline of the eye shape you have selected. Next, deepen the crease where the eyelid meets the eyebrow, and shape the curve of the eye. Finally, cut the second eye the same size as the first. Use calipers to take measurements of the first eye, if you feel strongly about the two eyes matching!

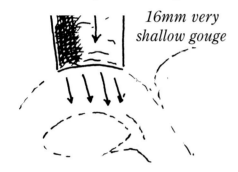

16mm very shallow gouge

11 Return to the bridge of the nose. Take a close look at the face so far. Are the eyes recessed enough? You should be able to clearly see the bridge above the eyeballs when viewing the carving from the side. If you cannot, remove some of the top of the eyeballs and recarve the eyes using skew and knife. The outside corners of the eyes should be lower than the inside corners.

12 With the straight gouge (16mm) or knife, cut away some of the areas below the eyes so that you have a smooth curve from the line below the eyes up onto the cheeks. Areas of cheeks will need to be cut down because the cheeks are not as high as the top-line of the nose. Check the profile of the face as you carve.

13 Draw the nostril edge of the nose (the base of the triangular nose shape). The nose probably won't be straight across the bottom, so draw the shape with as much contour as you wish. Is the nose long enough? Adjust the length if the eyes have taken too much cheek space and the nose is not long enough. Remember, an anatomically correct nose may be 1 to $1^1/2$ eye-widths in length.

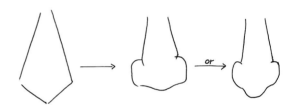

14 Make two or three cuts with the v-gouge to cut across the base of the nose. Refer to page 28 if the nose chips.

15 Using a knife or straight gouge, remove some bark below the nose in the area of the upper lip or where the mustache will be. The nose should be higher than any mustache, lip, or beard areas.

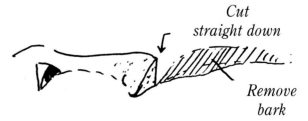

Cut straight down

Remove bark

16 Using a straight gouge (16 mm), cut straight down along the bottom edge of the nose on both sides. Use the two views below to help you plan your cuts

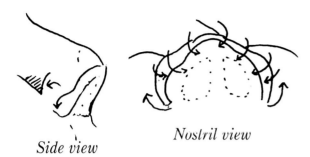

Side view   *Nostril view*

17 Using a knife and v-gouge, smooth and shape the nostrils. From the tip of the nose, slant the nostrils out and down. Refer to your own, in the mirror, if you need a model. Round the nostril edges where they meet the cheeks.

18 Shape the cheeks with a v-gouge, knife or very shallow round gouge. Start below the eyes, move along the nose, and down the upper lip area. Consider whether you wish to carve high cheek bones, rounded cheeks, sunken cheeks for a gaunt look, or other variations.

19 Return to the nose. Shape and refine width and general shape with a knife and skew. Smooth around the eyes with a knife. Refine the bridge of the nose and carry its shape, smoothly, on to the brow area using the knife and skew. At this point, stop to check the profile. Are all areas well-defined and strong?

20 Carve the lower face. Remember the tip of the nose protrudes farther than the mustache or lower-lip area. The lower lip probably does not protrude as far as the upper lip. Even when a mustache covers the top lip, recess the bottom lip sufficiently. If both lips are visible, curve them around the face; the corners are lower than the center of the lips. Line indentations from the corners of the lips to the outside edges of the nostrils separate the upper-lip area and the sides of the face. The upper lip may have a curved-line shape along the opening. A woman's lips will probably have a rounder shape than a man's lips.

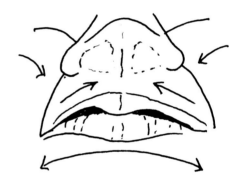

21 Finish cutting the beard lines. Use a variety of widths and lengths of lines to add the interest and indicate the flow of the hairs. The v-gouge will give a nice, "crisp" cut.

22 Review the entire face and profile. Using a knife and gouges, do the following:
- round any areas needing further work
- define shapes and contours and bring out personality
- cut top eye lids (and bottom, if desired)

If the bark does not chip too easily
- define any wrinkles
- add any extra details

24

23 Cut the nostrils in four steps.

(a) Make two knife cuts, one on each side of the septum but not as far as the nose tip.

(b) Start at the bottom and remove a small piece of bark in the nostril area.

(c) Work upward, with successive cuts, removing additional bark until the nostril is defined.

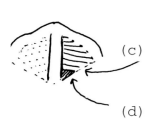

(d) Smooth the base of the upper lip area and inside the nostril. You do not need to cut deep nostrils. Cut the other nostril. If you have kept your knife and gouges very sharp and have worked over each area carefully, you should not have to do very much sanding.

24 Carve any additional features such as flowers and leaves; animal friends; special features that suggest pixies, gnomes, or leprechauns; faces surrounded by fruit, tree branches, or drapery; or special costumes.

Finishing

25 Cloth-backed sandpaper, sanding sticks, emery boards, and sandpaper wrapped around a wine bottle cork will all help you sand the details of the face. Use a fine grit sandpaper so that you do not mar the surface of the bark. You may also choose to burnish the wood to remove tiny marks. Use a burnisher, like the one shown below, or the back of a small teaspoon. Alternately, you may wish to let your knife cuts remain and not sand the piece.

As a rule of thumb, round the skin areas, but leave hair sharp and well-defined.

26 Sign, date and number your carving using a permanent felt marker.

27 On the back of the bark, drill a hole near the top so that the carving may be hung on the wall. Drill the hole in the thickest part of the upper section. The hole should not break through to the front. Using a v-gouge remove a "V" of wood starting about 1/4 inch below the drilled hole. Using your knife, smooth the edges of the hole.

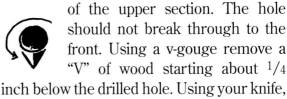

28 Paint the eyes or leave them natural.

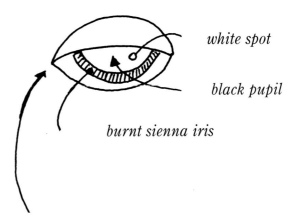

white spot

black pupil

burnt sienna iris

If you do not carve the top eyelid, draw a black line to simulate a "cut" line.

General Carving Instructions

29 Finish the face and the rough bark, or just the face, with a clear, low-luster or matte varnish. The varnish gives a finished look and enhances the grain pattern of the bark. But don't attempt to varnish the back and the front of the bark at the same time.

When applying varnish, be sure to read the manufacturer's directions and cautions carefully. Allow the first coat to dry thoroughly before deciding to apply a second coat. You may wish to try a number of varnishes. Some produce a livelier appearance and enhance the grain pattern better than others. The shine will mellow after a few days.

Recarve any trouble spots, then sand and varnish them again. If you don't like the shapes of the painted pupils, carve them away with a knife, sand, repaint, and varnish.

Bark carvings may also be painted with opaque colors, stained, or oiled.

30 Add any other materials. Polished stones, tiny chains, leather, feathers, gem stones, metal, and Tagua nuts are just a few examples of other items that can be added to a finished bark carving. The Wizard on page 32 holds a staff, why not a stone? Just hollow out a spot and glue in a stone of your choice. The illustration of a woman and her dog below shows how to incorporate a small chain.

FREE Pattern Offer!

YES! Please sign me up to receive a FREE scroll saw and/or woodcarving pattern.

☐ Woodcarving ☐ Scroll Saw

(Check your choice of pattern at right)

Previously purchased titles: _____

I'm particularly interested in: *(circle all that apply)*

General Woodworking   Woodcarving   Scroll Sawing   Cabinetmaking   Nature Drawing

Suggestion box:
I think Fox Chapel should do a book about: _____

BONUS! Give us your email address to receive more free patterns and updates!

Send to:

Name: _____   Email Address: _____

Address: _____

City: _____

State/Prov.: _____   Zip: _____

Country: _____

Visit us on the web at www.foxchapelpublishing.com

Fox
Chapel Publishing Co. Inc.

Free Pattern Offer
1970 Broad St.
East Petersburg PA 17520   USA

CHAPTER 6

"Help!" Solutions for Small Mishaps

Problem: Did you try to remove too much bark with one cut, and as a result, part of the face chipped off?

Solution:

(a) If you are using a very thick piece of bark, you may be able to cut the whole face deeper into the bark.

(b) Using wood glue, glue the chip back into place. Wood glue takes hours to "set" and dry, so secure the chip snugly using a rubber band. Tighten the band by placing a pill bottle or film canister under the rubber band on the back of the bark.

(c) This is the last chance to fix the cut before throwing the piece of bark on the firewood pile! If the "damaged" area can be carved away, it can be replaced by another, correctly carved section and glued in place. Use an identical piece of bark with the grain running the same direction.

Problem: Is the bark too brittle to carve?

Solution: Carve slowly with very little pressure. Simplify shapes and eliminate as many details, such as eyelids, as possible. Try spraying the face areas with water after you have removed the surface bark on the front and cover the area with plastic wrap for a day.

Problem: Did you find worm or larvae holes?

Solution: Clean the debris from the canal. Work down as deeply as you can. Finish carving and sanding the Cottonwood Spirit. Place the bark in the oven and heat it at about 225° F for at least half an hour. (If you smell scorching wood, your oven is too hot! Remove the bark before you have a fire!) Any remaining creatures should be dead now.

Cool the bark. Fill the canal with wood filler. Allow the filler to dry thoroughly and then sand. Bark sawdust mixed with glue may also be used to fill the hole. Using acrylic Raw Sienna, paint the filler. This color should be a satisfactory match, but you

"Help!"

may have to experiment a bit. Continue with normal finishing of the bark.

Problem: Are there cracks in the bark?
Solution: The best procedure is to avoid carving a face over a crack. Cracks are quite pleasing in beards and hair, etc. but if they run through eyes, top lips, or noses, fill them with wood filler. Allow the filler time to dry thoroughly, then paint it with Raw Sienna acrylic paint (or a paint mix that simulates the color of the bark).

If you can't avoid carving facial features over a crack, use a profile. Also, try to incorporate the crack into your carving. Cracks lend a lot of interest to a carving if they fall in the natural areas of the bark.

Problem: Does the interior, brown color of the bark show in spots on bark areas that you wish to leave "au natural?"
Solution: Sometimes when removing bark from the tree, other ribs may pull pieces of bark away or break a surface. Wire brushing or accidental gouge and knife slips may mar the bark, too.

(a) Paint the affected area with a couple of thin washes of acrylic. Often, thin Paynes Grey will suffice, but you may want to mix colors. Allow the paint to dry before varnishing the bark.

(b) Paint all the rough bark areas with a coat of acrylic. A white-grey or a darker brown is pleasing.

(c) If the exposed area is rough due to a broken rib, carve it smooth, then finish it as you would the rest of the bark or face.

(d) Don't do anything! Spots of interior bark that are the same color as the face do not detract from the general appearance of the finished work!

Problem: Did the top of the nose chip off when you carved the nostrils?
Solution: Glue it on! Next time avoid any upward pressure as you cut the nostril openings.

Problem: Did your black marker run when you applied the varnish?
Solution: Allow the varnish time to dry. Using the very shallow round gouge (16 mm) or plane, remove the affected area. Sand if necessary. Find a *permanent* black marker and sign again. Revarnish. The acrylic Paynes Grey paint won't run, if you don't mind writing with a fine brush and paint.

Problem: Did the "ribs" come apart?
Solution: Sometimes only the thin back layer holds ribs together. When you remove it, you have two (or more) separate carvings!

Glue the pieces together along the break line. Then, take a strip of brown fabric about 1 1/2 inches wide and put glue on both sides. Press it on the back over the crack. Hold the bark sections together, firmly, with elastic bands or string. Be sure the ribs are flat and touch each other in the same places they originally did! Allow the glue to thoroughly dry before continuing.

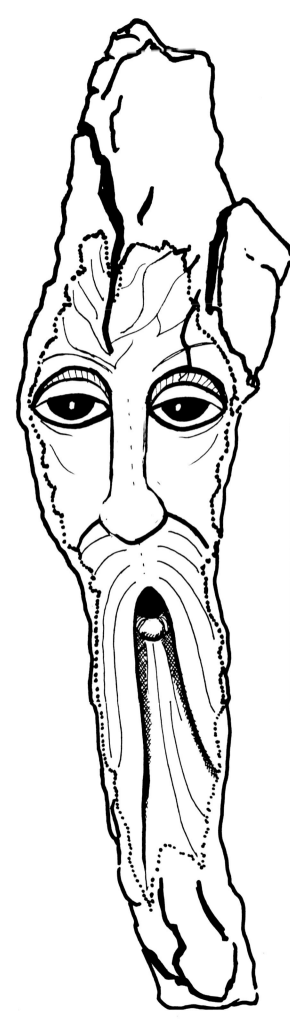

Ancient Cottonwood Sage

Many pieces of bark seem to best lend themselves to the carving of one face. This piece, with a wider section near the top and a thinner section below it, was well suited to carving a face with a long beard.

As I thought about the possibilities for this piece of bark, an ancient sage with tired, serious eyes and a long beard came to mind.

This piece of bark has two cracks near the top. I placed the eyes just below them. Cracks through the eyes are troubling to the viewer and disfigure a face. Cracks in the hair, beard, mustache or outer edges are less disturbing.

This Sage's mustache and long beard eliminate a top lip area, which a beginning carver may find difficult to carve.

An Ancient Cottonwood Sage

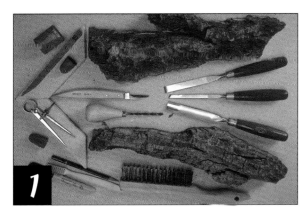

Tools and two pieces of bark. The rough exterior of the bark has not been removed. Both pieces of bark will work well for the Sage.

Remove the rough surface of the back with the straight gouge. Wire-brush the front and decide how much of the rough bark will remain. With the flat gouge, remove the bark in the face area. Curve the surface in a convex shape. Mark the eyebrows, nose and mouth lines.

Using the v-gouge cut along both sides of the nose. Shape the eyebrows with the large shallow gouge. Mark the lines below the eyes.

Lower the bridge of the nose. With a v-gouge cut across under the eyes. Shape the eyes with a skew, knife, or straight gouge.

Measure the width of the eyes. Use calipers if you wish to make identically sized eyes. Measure horizontally and vertically. Turn your work around so that you view it from a different direction to help you to detect discrepancies between the right and left sides.

Using the eye-width measurement, mark the length of the nose—about one-and-one-half times the width of the eye. Cut the base of the nose in a wide "V" shape and cut straight down the nostril-opening surface. Use a flat gouge.

Cut away the area below the nose. Refine the outer shape of the nose, cheeks, and flare of the nostrils. Drill a round hole where the opening of the mouth will be.

With knife and v-gouge, cut the line of the mustache. Shape the bottom lip. Remember to curve it under the mustache.

Make "V" cuts for the flow of the hair. Cut the eyebrows and nostrils and smooth any rough areas with a knife and gouges.

Sand areas and make any last minute alterations. Check to be sure the inside corners of the eyes are exactly opposite each other. Sharpen the mouth and hair lines again. Be sure all tool marks have been sanded off. Finish.

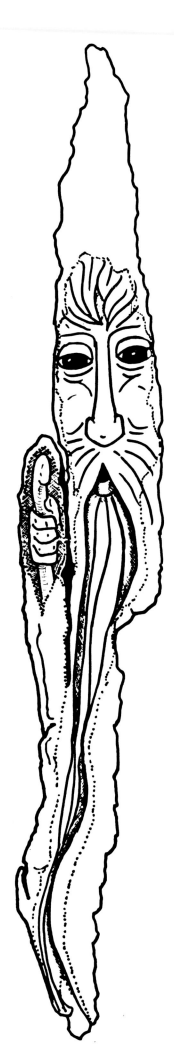

Cottonwood Wizard

Thick bark is desirable because it allows for a stronger, wider relief carving. However, it is not necessary! Bark less than one inch thick and 2 inches wide can be carved. The thin bark has the same variety of contour lines as the larger barks. You will be limited in size, depth, and width, but many interesting faces can be carved! Often the smaller ribs are long elliptical shapes pointed at the top and bottom. These points allow for impressions of conical hats and long pointed beards—perfect for a wizard.

Carving Thin Pieces of Bark

• When removing the rough bark on the front surface, carve straight across. Try to allow for a small amount of convex curve, but you will not have much.

• Trace the shape of your bark onto a piece of paper and draw the face, to the correct size, onto your piece of paper.

• Follow the general carving instructions in Chapter 5. Modify these so that you do not carve completely through the depth of bark!

• Sometimes an extra "rib" may be part of the one you've carved the face into, as was the case in the piece I used. It suggested a hand holding a cane to me. Use your imagination and add details to your carving.

Lady of the Cottonwoods

The shape of this bark may tempt one to carve a man's face with a long beard but you can also find the faces of Cottonwood ladies, too. Because the bark is narrow, the full-face will need to be slim with a profile carved below it.

When carving the profile, remember that the cheek will be the highest area. Using a v-gouge, cut

the curved cheek line first. The outside of the nostril and the eye are the next highest areas. The tip of the nose is not as high as the outer edge of the nostril.

Only half of the eye needs to be seen in profiles. When the bark is narrow and a profile is being carved, it may be necessary to allow long hair to partly cover the face.

Retaining the rough outer bark on the edges of the carving adds interest to the carving. The bark cannot be mistaken for any other wood if you leave some of the bark's surface on the carving.

Lady of the Cottonwoods

Tools and bark. The wider top section suggested a full-face view while the narrower bottom section was more suited to a profile (half-face).

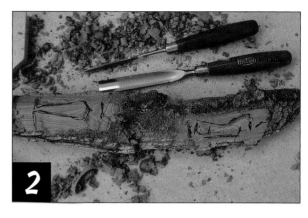

Remove surface bark with a straight gouge and round the top face. The bottom section, where the profile will be, is convexly shaped only on the "face" side. With a pencil, mark facial features. Using a v-gouge, define the sides of the noses. Cut the eyebrows, noses, and eyes.

Measure the width of the eye using calipers. When placing the eyes on the top lady, make both eyes identically sized.

Use the eye measurement to establish the length of the nose (about one-and-one-half eye widths). Measure the top lady's eye width and establish the nose in the same way.

On the top lady, remove the excess bark on the top-lip area with a knife or straight gouge. Cut the curve of the cheek and the lower edge of the nose, top lip, and chin areas on the profile.

Cut the mouth and lower lip areas of the profile (these are half the full-face). Curve the cheek down, onto the nose, lips, and chin.

7

Remove more outer bark as needed below the full-face mouth to allow for the flow of hair and the indentation below the chin.

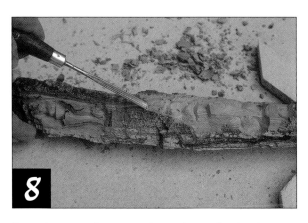

8

If you have small gouges, the neck may be deeply recessed. Do not remove too much of the bark if you will be unable to carve it smoothly.

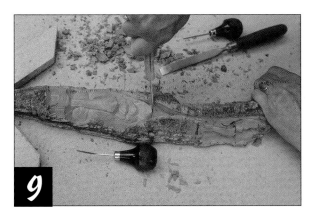

9

Smooth the hairline from the top figure onto the forehead of the bottom figure. [These brown-handled gouges are "micro" gouges used for miniature carving. The yellow handled tool is a palm-held v-gouge.]

10

Using the knife, cut the indentations in the sides of the nose and shape the outside of the nostrils. Then cut the openings of the nostrils.

11

Define the hairline of the bottom figure and recess the neck area. Be sure the "flow" will be smooth between the chin and the neck.

12

Smooth and sand any rough areas. Paint the eyes and finish.

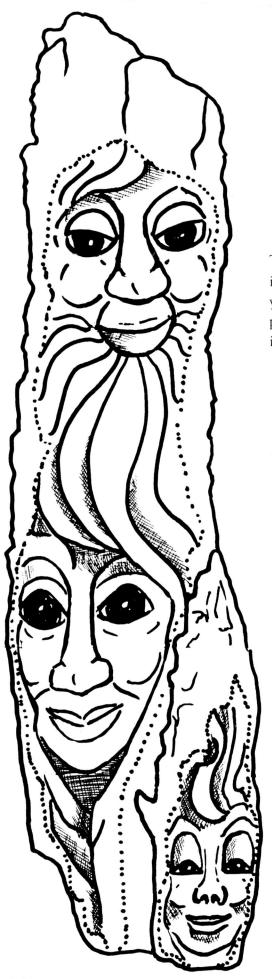

Cottonwood Trio

The two ribs of your bark may not be fastened together in the same place as these are, so arrange the faces to fit your piece. You may wish to enlarge any or all. (See page 12 for information on enlarging and reducing illustrations.)

Carving Facial Expressions

• A variety in facial expression is more interesting. As time has progressed, I have gravitated toward happier faces.

• Whiskers cover a lot of facial detail, and you may find beards easier to carve than the mouths and chins. Because of this, you may wish to carve only male features.

• The top figure's face is more like a dwarf's, and you might like to pursue that type further. Find pictures of dwarfs' faces and incorporate their features into your carvings.

• If you wish to carve a more child-like face than the little ones in this carving, you will find that children's faces have wide foreheads, larger eyes, less space between the eyebrows and chin, rounder cheeks, and a shorter nose.

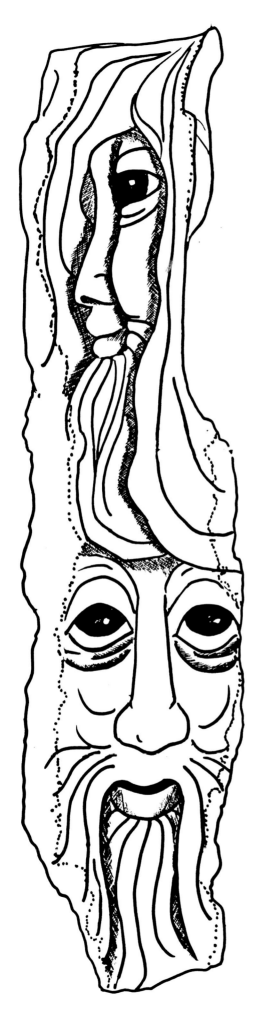

Two Grand Masters

The Two Grand Masters, probably with long beards and "tired" eyes, will fit nicely on a piece of bark of this size. However, as in Lady of the Cottonwoods, one section of the bark is noticeably narrower. A profile will offer the best solution for the narrow section.

Carving Faces in Profile

• Carve the cheek-line, of the profile, before beginning the rest of the face. Continually be aware of which areas are recessed more deeply.

• Encourage the viewer's eyes to travel smoothly from the profile to the bottom face with long flowing hair lines.

Because the faces are close together, the beard of the profile can become the forehead hair of the lower face.

• The eyes look upward so that the lower face forms a link with the profile.

• Note that the eyes are cut differently in this carving. With the v-gouge, outline the top eyelid then outline the semi-circle shape of the pupil. Then use a knife and carve the "white" of the eye lower than the pupil. Carve the pupil a bit lower than the eyelid. Make a small hole where the "light spot" will be on the pupil. (The point of the knife may be used.) Sand and shape the edges.

Two Grand Masters

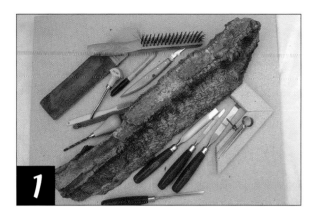

This 21-inch piece of bark is nearly five inches wide and four inches thick .

Bottom Face: Using a v-gouge, outline the nose and carve the eyebrows (use the very shallow round gouge). Top Profile: Use the v-gouge to carve the cheek-line then the line below the eye. Lower the nose leaving the cheek higher. Use the knife, skew, and straight gouge.

Cut the eye-shapes with a v-gouge, knife, and skew and measure the widths. Your measurements will be more accurate if you use calipers.

The nose will be about one-and-one-half eye-widths long. Mark a wide "V" at its base. Note that the nostril area is wider than the bridge of the nose.

Carve and shape the cheek areas with the knife and round gouges and remove some bark below the nose. Cut the nostril areas straight down with a straight gouge. Mark the beard lines.

Repeat these same steps (as for previous photo) on the profile. Begin with the v-gouge and outline the cheek-line, then proceed with gouges and a knife to remove bark in the lowered areas.

Carve the upper and lower lips on the profile with a knife. Remove excess bark, if needed.

Remove more of the side, rough bark to give a convex flow. Carve the mouth line and remove more bark in the bottom lip and center beard area with the knife and gouge.

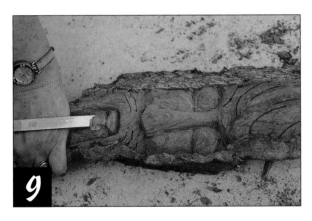

Shape the bottom lip, remembering to recess the sides under the mustache. Remove more bark from the beard (below the bottom lip) with the straight gouge.

Cut the lines of the beards with the v-gouge. Smooth and cut the outside shape of the nostrils and cut the nostril holes. Carve the eyes. Review all curved areas, modifying any and carving all as smoothly as you can using a knife.

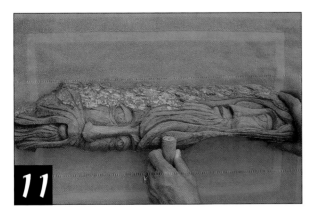

Sand the carving using the cork-and-sandpaper for the flat areas and curves. For narrow areas, fold a sheet of sand paper to make a point, if you do not have a sandpaper stick.

Apply varnish (if this is your choice of finish). Remember to read the manufacturer's directions carefully and wait the recommended time for the varnish to dry. Allow one side to dry before doing the other side.

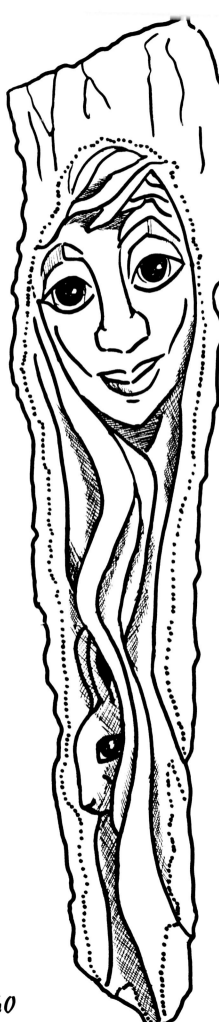

Youthful Cottonwood Spirit

Although the bark sections suggest a vertical placement, the face may be angled to create a more dynamic carving. As these are imaginary spirits, a strict adherence to symmetry is not necessary. Capturing the feeling or mood is more important.

The soft curving lines of the girl's hair and the variety of lengths of the strands give a more feminine impression.

The rabbit has been included to add interest to an otherwise long line of hair.

Carving a Feminine Face

Carve:
• A more pointed chin
• Full well-curved lips
• Large attractive eyes
• Well-curved eyebrows
• Curving hairline
• Smooth lines curving from the cheek to the chin

Cottonwood Duo

An unusually shaped piece of bark offers an interesting challenge. No two pieces are ever quite the same. Because this piece is not very long, it is more difficult to carve two faces. The solution will be to have the second face , a lady, peering out from under the old man's beard. She can be placed right at the bottom with her chin along the bottom edge.

The long flowing lines of the irregular bark on the left side add interest to the hair and beard of the top figure. Sometimes irregular projections aren't where you might wish! The right side irregularities point upward, but will not be removed. They add interest. The viewer's imagination can determine what they are!

Cottonwood Duo

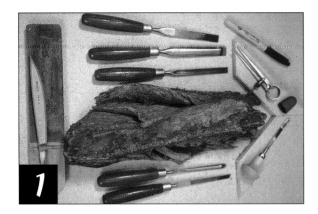

Note the piece of very thick bark. It came from a mountain valley where there is abundant rainfall. The dead stump is huge! This is a piece of bark of unusual shape. You will probably not find one like it, so plan your carving on a long rectangular piece.

Clean the back with a plane or very shallow round gouge and wire-brush the front. Remove the top surface of the front with the straight gouge. With a pencil or felt pen mark guidelines for the brow, nose, mouth and flow of beard.

Using the v-gouge define the sides of the nose, eyebrows and cuts under the eyes. Do this to both faces. Working on both together will enable you to see how the lines of one flow into the other.

The bottom figure's face needs to be cut well into the bark so that she appears to be behind the beard of the top figure. After shaping the nose with the v-gouge, determine its length and cut along the nostril line.

Return to the upper face and establish the nose length. Define the eye shape with a knife or round gouges. Cut away excess bark from the upper lip area with a knife or straight gouge, and carve the mouth and lower lip.

Shape the chin and nostrils of the lower figure. Carve the mouth line and lower lip. Use a knife and round gouges. On the upper figure, remove some bark between the mustache lines with the v-gouge. Cut the mustache lines deeper and match the cuts to the cracks.

Cut the beard lines with the v-gouge. Smooth areas more carefully, then cut the nostrils with the knife.

Define the eyebrows and the upper figure's hairline using v-gouge, knife, and round gouges.

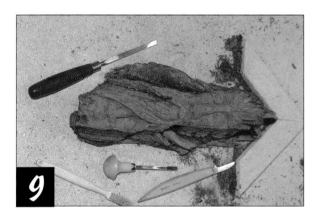

Sand all areas and make any adjustments in line cuts. Top Figure: Straighten mouth line, cut lips thinner, deepen "V" cuts, check symmetry of eyes. Bottom Figure: Raise mouth line 1/4", shape chin. Sanding dust will be allowed to fill the crack in the chin and varnish will be applied over it.

Paint the eyes. The placement of the pupils will determine the direction of the gaze.

A low-luster clear varnish will enhance the grain in the bark. One coat is usually sufficient. Allow the varnish to dry thoroughly, then decide whether you wish to apply a second coat.

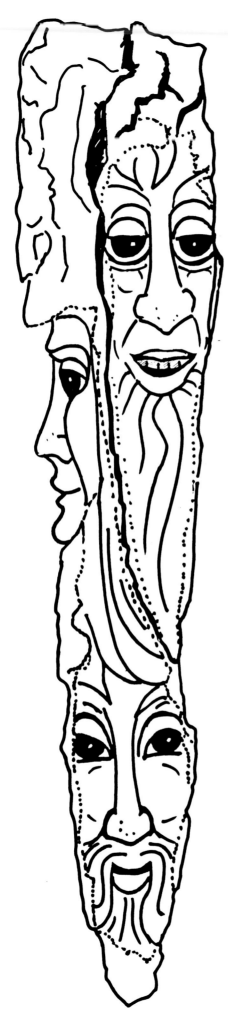

Cottonwood Smiles and Chuckles

Two full-face views and a side view fit nicely on a two-ribbed piece of bark. You probably will not find one like this, but you may organize these faces to fit a piece of bark you do have.

Using paper, trace around your piece of bark. Decide where the faces will fit. Allow natural (exterior) bark to show along most edges. The dotted line on my pattern indicates the separation between the carved area and the outside bark.

Carving Multiple Figures

• A variety of heights will look best. Try to avoid the facial features of one being on the same level with those of another.

• Allow hair, or beards, to flow down so that your eye follows easily from one face to another.

• Cut facial features differently. Variety adds interest unless you specifically want a look of "oneness" to all the faces!

• Try to avoid bark "cracks" in crucial areas. Retaining the natural bark on the outer edges, and even along cracks, enhances the appearance of your carving. If the natural bark is very clean, solid, and contrasts well with the color of the carved area, you may wish to "finish" only the face areas.

44